Look at an Ash Tree

by Patricia M. Stockland

first step nonfiction

Lerner Publications Company · Minneapolis

root

This is a root of an
ash tree.

This is a trunk of an
ash tree.

branch

This is a branch of an
ash tree.

4

leaf

This is a leaf of an
ash tree.

seed

This is a seed of an ash tree.

This is an ash tree!

The images in this book are used with the permission of: © Len Wilcox/Alamy, p. 2; © Erin Paul Donovan/SuperStock, p. 3; © Age Fotostock/SuperStock, p. 4; © iStockphoto.com/ AnkNet, p. 5; © iStockphoto.com/Ruud de Man, p. 6; © GAP/SuperStock, p. 7. Front cover: © Todd Pearson/Photographer's Choice/Getty Images.

Lerner Publications Company
A division of Lerner Publishing Group, Inc.
241 First Avenue North
Minneapolis, MN 55401 U.S.A.

Website address: www.lernerbooks.com

Main body text set in ITC Avant Garde Gothic Std 21/25.
Typeface provided by International Typeface Corp.

Library of Congress Cataloging-in-Publication Data

Stockland, Patricia M.
    Look at an ash tree / by Patricia M. Stockland.
        p.   cm. — (First step nonfiction. Look at trees)
    Ash tree
    ISBN 978–1–4677–0526–4 (pbk. : alk. paper)
    1. Ash (Plants)—Juvenile literature. I. Title. II. Title: Ash tree. III. Series: Stockland, Patricia M. First step nonfiction. Look at trees.
SD397.A6S86 2013
635.9'77—dc23   2012013237

Manufactured in the United States of America
1 – BP – 7/15/12